CONTENTS

Words appearing in the text in bold, **like this**, are explained in the glossary.

AN INSPIRATIONAL POET

Roger McGough has won awards for writing plays, songs, and films. He has been a popstar at the top of the charts. He is also a respected broadcaster on television and radio. However, first and foremost, he has had an amazing career as a poet. In the 1960s, his fresh, fun performances helped to change many people's perception of poetry. He turned poetry from an old-fashioned art form, stuck in the past, into popular modern entertainment.

Roger has remained one of the best-loved British poets for adults but has also become a firm favourite with children too. Thousands of young people have delighted in poetry collections such as *Bad Bad Cats*, **anthologies** such as *Strictly Private*, and stories such as *Stinkers Ahoy!* and *Dotty Inventions*. His effortless style has inspired countless fans to pick up a pen themselves.

The person behind the poetry.

4

What is Roger like?

Do you recognise Roger? You might have watched him give a poetry reading or seen him on television. He is tall and thin. When he was younger, he was into all sorts of fashions, including wearing military jackets and berets (in the 1960s), furry afghan coats (in the 1970s), and having a ponytail and an earring (in the 1980s). Today, he sticks to plainer clothes, but he still enjoys wearing a colourful pair of green-framed glasses, an earring, and a goatee beard. In normal conversation, Roger talks very quietly and very quickly, so it is sometimes difficult to catch what he is saying. But when he performs, he is vibrant – full of emotion and energy!

FIND OUT MORE...

Here are some of Roger's favourites:

Favourite food...	Italian
Favourite TV show...	*Match of the Day*
Favourite football team...	Everton
Favourite hobby...	reading, going out with friends
Favourite music...	a little of everything and not too much of anything (but Roger especially likes The Beatles)
Favourite animal...	Birds
Favourite writer...	Roger has many favourite writers, but some that have particularly influenced him are Dylan Thomas, Adrian Mitchell, and James Joyce.
Favourite saying...	"Amen"

Roger was born on 9 November 1937. His parents lived in the city of Liverpool, in a suburb called Seaforth. He was named after his father, who worked at the big, busy docks at the mouth of the River Mersey. His mother's name was Mary. Two years after Roger was born, the couple had a daughter called Brenda.

Roger's home

The McGough family lived at 11 Ruthven Road. It was a small house sandwiched into a long **terrace** of others. All the people in the street knew everyone else, so it was a friendly neighbourhood and there were lots of children for Roger to play with. Both Roger's father and mother came from big families. Lots of uncles and aunties, as well as his grandparents, often popped in and out.

The little boy who was to grow up and become famous.

A wartime childhood

Roger was a small child during World War II, which lasted from 1939 to 1945. Liverpool was often bombed by the Germans, but Roger was too young to understand what was happening or to be scared. He was regularly whisked off in the middle of the night to an air-raid shelter, but instead of finding it terrifying, Roger thought it was exciting.

FIND OUT MORE...

Life in Liverpool and other big cities during the war was so dangerous that many children were sent to stay with families in the countryside. When Roger was four, his mother took him and his sister Brenda to North Wales. They missed Liverpool and, after a few months, they returned home. Luckily they remained unharmed, even though the end of their road was blown to bits.

During the war, children who were sent away from their homes in cities to safer places were called evacuees.

Playtime

Roger spent a lot of time outdoors with friends, playing in their yards or going scavenging over the rubble of destroyed homes. Sometimes they stood and watched **prisoners-of-war** who were sent to work knocking down half-bombed, unsafe buildings. Roger and his friends would come back later and explore the ruins.

Many children loved hunting for useful things on bomb sites.

Prayer time

Roger's family were strong believers in God. They were Roman Catholics who went to church regularly. Roger became an altar boy – a priest's helper at **Mass**. He developed a firm Catholic faith, which has stayed with him all his life.

Roger in his school uniform with his sister, Brenda, and their mother, Mary. Unfortunately Mary's head is not in the picture!

School days

Roger's first school was the local primary in Seaforth, called Star of the Sea. Roger's mother thought that getting a good education was very important, and wanted her children to go to the best schools. She was delighted when Roger passed the entrance exam for a good prviate school, called St Mary's **Prep School**.

Roger's parents worked hard to afford the school fees. His mother took on part-time work, such as at the Lincolnshire Laundry in Stoneycroft, which was owned by her family. Roger did well at his school work and passed the exam to go to a grammar school called St Mary's College. He even won an entrance prize called a **scholarship**.

INSIDE INFORMATION

When Roger was a young boy, his mother taught him lots of nursery rhymes and fairy tales. This inspired his love of **rhythm** and rhyme, and encouraged a vivid imagination. It also influenced the talent for poetry that he developed as he grew older.

Performing poetry

Roger found life at St Mary's College stiff and strict. Poetry was taught from an old-fashioned anthology called *Palgrave's Golden Treasury*, and Roger found all the poems dull, dry, and boring. He liked more modern poems with action in them, like Lewis Carroll's *Jabberwocky* and John Masefield's *Cargoes*. Roger discovered that he was very good at **reciting** this sort of poetry aloud. At the age of twelve, he entered a verse-reading competition and won.

Jabberwocky comes from Lewis Carroll's Through the Looking Glass.

FIND OUT MORE...

Roger had private lessons in **elocution**. This was because his mother thought that he spoke too quickly, running all his words together. Today, as a top poet, Roger is a lively performer of his work.

Books, not boxing!

Roger's father wanted him to be good at sport. He bought Roger boxing gloves for his thirteenth birthday and encouraged Roger to play in the school cricket team. However, Roger was more interested in drama, music, and books. He was excellent at acting in school plays, and he took violin lessons and sang in the school choir. Like all teenage boys of the time, Roger enjoyed popular comics such as *Wizard*, *Hotspur*, and *Rover*. He loved good reads such as the adventure story *Treasure Island* by Robert Louis Stevenson, and classic novels like *A Tale of Two Cities* by Charles Dickens. English was Roger's best school subject, but surprisingly he failed his **'O' Level** exam! Instead, in the sixth form, he studied French, History, and Geography.

Roger aged 17 with his sister, mother and father on holiday in Linlithgow, Scotland.

OFF INTO THE WORLD

When Roger finished school, he went on to Hull University. It was exciting to live away from home for the first time, in a students' **hall of residence**. Roger met all sorts of interesting people. He was studying for a degree in French and Geography. However, he also developed a burning desire to express himself in some kind of creative way.

First, Roger tried music. He played a **tea-chest bass** in a student group called Tinhorn Timmins and the Rattlesnakes. Then he tried art and spent many long nights experimenting with painting. Next, Roger began composing poetry. He was eighteen years old, and it was the first time he had ever had a go at writing anything. He kept his poems secret, and spent lots of time working hard on them.

Here is Roger with his cricket team. He is sitting in the front row, second from the right.

HAVE A GO

If you want to write poetry, you could begin like Roger did. He started by stealing forms, rhythms and language styles from poets he admired, such as Baudelaire (a French poet), TS Eliot, Wilfred Owen, GM Hopkins, and Dylan Thomas. Gradually, he found his own poetic "voice" and did not need to steal ideas any more.

Important influences

Roger discovered that the **warden** of his hall of residence, and the head librarian of the university library, was a top poet called Philip Larkin. After a long time being shy, Roger plucked up courage and showed Larkin some of his poems. Roger was thrilled, because Larkin was encouraging and supportive. Then Roger went to hear the poet Christopher Logue give a reading. Roger thought Logue's poems and performance were wonderful. He made up his mind that he also wanted to be a poet more than anything else.

The famous poet, Philip Larkin. A collection of his poems published in 1964, called The Whitsun Weddings, won the Queen's Gold Medal for Poetry.

Earning a living

Roger had to think about what to do after university. He knew it was almost impossible to earn a living from poetry. After all, even the famous Philip Larkin had to have a job and write in his spare time. Roger decided that he could be a teacher, while continuing to work hard on his poems.

After graduating, Roger studied for a year to get a teaching qualification. Then, aged 22, Roger returned to Liverpool to teach French, Geography and Drama at a boys' school called St Kevin's. After a few years, he moved to an unusual job at Mabel Fletcher College. It allowed Roger to indulge his love of language, because it involved teaching **catering** students all about the French words that appeared on menus, and also teaching English. All the time, Roger kept writing poetry.

Roger the assistant lecturer at Mabel Fletcher Technical College. He is sitting on the front row, second from the left.

Café society

In the 1960s in Liverpool's city centre, there were many café bars and clubs where young musicians, painters, and writers met up. Roger hung out in these creative places, and became good friends with two other poets: a lecturer at Manchester College of Art called Adrian Henri and a young journalist named Brian Patten. They shared a passion for writing poetry about everyday Liverpool life, in down-to-earth language. The three started to read their poems in coffee bars and pubs, where bands played too. Their readings were not serious and stuffy; they were lively, fun performances that involved the audience. They were great entertainment.

FIND OUT MORE...

From the early 1960s, a band called The Beatles took the world by storm. They came from Liverpool, so they drew people's attention towards the city and its exciting artistic scene.

The Beatles were Paul McCartney, John Lennon, Ringo Starr, and George Harrison..

New developments

In 1963, Roger fell in love with Thelma Monaghan, a painter and designer who also ran a fashion boutique. Roger soon moved in with Thelma and her three-year-old son, Nathan. He was still teaching and also performing poems, everywhere from small basement gatherings to big arts festivals in Liverpool and Edinburgh.

In 1964, a television producer saw one of Roger's shows and invited him to be part of a programme called *Gazette*. Roger gave up teaching and joined a small group of performers creating funny sketches, songs, and poems. They called themselves The Scaffold. They appeared on other television programmes, such as *The Eleventh Hour*, and also toured around the country. Roger developed some sketches into theatre plays, including *Birds, Marriages and Deaths*. He often acted in the plays he wrote, and appeared in television dramas such as *Saturday While Sunday*.

The Scaffold was made up of John Gorman, Roger McGough, and Mike McCartney (who liked to be known as Mike McGear).

Sudden success

After three hectic years, The Scaffold slowed down. Roger taught part-time at Liverpool College of Art and enjoyed working on his poetry. In March 1967, Roger's poems appeared in an anthology called *The Liverpool Scene*. Then in May, a company called Penguin produced an anthology written purely by Roger, Adrian, and Brian, called *The Mersey Sound*. It became a bestseller.

Just a month later, Roger had a poetry collection, called *Summer with Monika*, published with a novel, called *Frink*. In October 1967, The Scaffold had a huge hit record with a song called *Thank U Very Much*. Roger was suddenly a pop star. Best of all, people were praising him as a poet.

INSIDE INFORMATION

Like Roger, Brian Patten and Adrian Henri both had many more books published and became top poets. Adrian is a favourite with young readers for fun collections such as *Rhinestone Rhino*.

Brian, Roger and Adrian (from left to right) remained friends. Together, they were known as "the Mersey sound".

ROGER THE POET

Roger had gone from rising star to famous household name. Theatre, radio, and television companies started to ask him to write plays. Roger became involved with writing a film script, *The Yellow Submarine*, for superstars The Beatles. The Scaffold had another pop hit with *Lily the Pink* and performed at royal gala shows and on television specials. However, first and foremost, Roger wrote poetry. Another collection, *Watchwords*, was published in 1969.

New commitments

In 1970, Roger and Thelma finally got married, in a quiet ceremony. In 1972, Thelma gave birth to a baby boy, Finn, and two years later to another son, Tom. The Scaffold had broken up by now, and Thelma hoped that Roger might be at home more. However his life was still a whirl of performing and poetry.

Roger was part of a new poetry/sketch/song group called Grimms. He also taught part-time as Poetry Fellow at Loughborough University, and he worked hard on his writing, producing four more poetry collections between 1970 and 1974. Roger also became a presenter for an educational children's TV programme called *Focus*. He thought of all sorts of ideas to make school subjects interesting – of course, they often involved poetry! It was the first time Roger had created something especially for a young audience.

In the film *The Yellow Submarine*, The Beatles go on a mission to save Pepperland from music-hating enemies called the Blue Meanies.

FIND OUT MORE...

Grimms was thought up by John Gorman, Andy Roberts, Neil Innes, Roger McGough, Mike McGear, and Vivian Stanshall. They formed the name of the group from the initial letters of their surnames. Other musicians and writers also contributed, including Adrian Henri, Brian Patten, and Zoot Money.

Making a move

Roger and Thelma grew apart, and in 1975 the couple split up. Roger began spending more time in London, working as a presenter on the television programme *Book Tower*. He also put together a poetry collection called *In the Glassroom*, toured abroad, and continued to give readings and appear at festivals all over Britain.

Roger was back in his home town of Liverpool one day, waiting at a bus stop, when he got talking to Hilary Clough, who was a lecturer at a college in Liverpool. The two began going out together, and when Hilary moved to London to further her studies, Roger went with her. The couple soon settled into a flat in a part of the capital city with a famous, fascinating market, called Portobello Road.

Portobello Road was a trendy, exciting place to live.

A brand new type of book

One day, a publisher friend suggested to Roger that he should try writing books for children. Roger used an idea behind *The Scaffold's* final song, *Mr Noselighter*, to write a story-poem about a man with a candle for a nose. It was published as a picture book in 1977. Roger continued to write poetry and plays for adults, but now he was also inspired to reach a younger audience. In 1979, a publisher produced a collection of children's poems written by Roger and another poet, Michael Rosen. It was called *You Tell Me*. In 1981, Roger put together an anthology of other poets' work for teenagers to enjoy, entitled *Strictly Private*.

Michael Rosen has since become a favourite young people's poet, like Roger. His books include the hilarious *Quick, Let's Get Out Of Here!*

Mr. Noselighter

By Roger McGough
Illustrated by André François

Mr Noselighter was Roger's first picture book for children, published in 1977.

From strength to strength

In the early 1980s, all sorts of writing poured from Roger's pen. He created several plays for the theatre, including one he wrote jointly with Brian Patten. It was called *The Mouthtrap*, and it was about poets and poetry. Roger and Brian starred in it too, at the Tricycle and Lyric theatres in London and at the Edinburgh Fringe Festival. Roger also wrote plays for radio, such as *Walking the Dog*, and did **screenwriting** for television, including a documentary called *Hope Street Glory*. He had new collections of poetry for adults published, such as *Unlucky for Some* and *Waving at Trains*.

However, Roger found himself having more and more ideas for children's books. In 1982, he had another storybook published, called *The Great Smile Robbery*. Roger and his publisher put lots of effort into the look of the book, because they wanted to make it as lively as one of Roger's poetry performances.

The words and letters in *The Great Smile Robbery* were arranged in unexpected, exciting ways, and the pages were covered with lots of funny line illustrations by Tony Blundell. Young readers especially loved some revolting characters called the Stinkers.

INSIDE INFORMATION

Roger did not begin *The Great Smile Robbery* with the Stinkers in mind. He invented the gruesome gang as he was writing the tale. Roger never starts a story with a fully-formed plot or characters. He sets out from just a spark of an idea and sees what happens as he goes along.

Writing, writing – and more writing!

Roger wrote more children's stories, such as *The Stowaways*; picture books such as *The Kite and Caitlin*; funny information books such as *Until I Met Dudley*; and lots of poetry collections such as *Sky in the Pie*, *An Imaginary Menagerie*, *Bad Bad Cats*, *Sensational*, and *Wicked Poems*. He also created theatre plays for young people, such as *The Sound Collector* and *My Dad's A Fire Eater*, and found himself in high demand as an **editor** of anthologies. Of course, he continued with all sorts of writing for adults. He was also regularly asked to appear on television and radio programmes. Somehow in all this whirl of activity, Roger found time to marry Hilary. In 1986 they had a son, Matthew, and in 1990 they had a daughter, Isabel.

23

Being Roger McGough

Today, Roger and his family live in Barnes, West London. As one of the most famous, best-selling poets in Britain, he is always kept very busy with broadcasting work, giving interviews, making public appearances at events around the country, and going on tours abroad. Roger also makes sure that he meets his young fans on regular school visits and book-signings at bookshops. He really enjoys giving readings of his work, particularly to family audiences. Roger is out and about so often nowadays that it can be difficult for him to find time to write! However, composing poetry is still what he enjoys doing most of all.

Barnes is on the River Thames. Roger likes it because it has a village atmosphere but it is only five miles from central London.

As a writer, Roger spends a lot of time shut away on his own. To relax, he likes going out with his family and friends for a meal or to the pub.

Roger at home

Roger is an intriguing person. Having spent his life surrounded by poetry and music, you might think that he would have a big collection of books and CDs at home. In fact, although Roger loves reading, most of the books in his house belong to Hilary. Roger does not buy much music either, because he cannot work with music playing. Roger has written many poems for young people about animals, especially cats. However, although the family always has a pet cat or two, Roger is not a cat-lover in particular. In fact, for many years he had a beloved dog, Bran – the son of popstar Paul McCartney's dog, Martha!

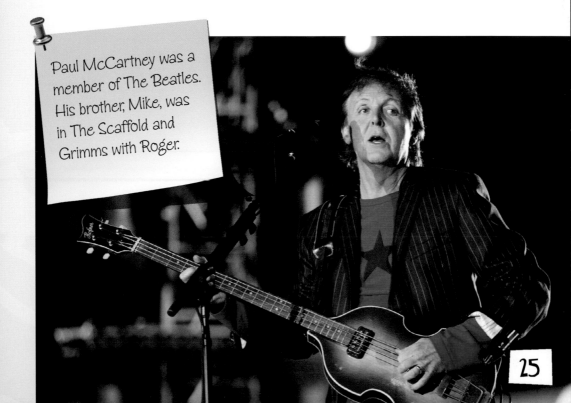

Paul McCartney was a member of The Beatles. His brother, Mike, was in The Scaffold and Grimms with Roger.

ROGER'S WORK

Roger has an untidy, but comfortable, study in which he does all his writing. There is a large desk, countless pencils and pens and notebooks, and a huge wastepaper basket. Roger keeps several reference books within easy reach, including *The Collins English Dictionary*, *Roget's Thesaurus*, and *The Poet's Manual and Rhyming Dictionary*. He also likes having **rosary beads** and dental floss to hand.

Roger's life as a writer is not neat and organized. Whenever he is working on a particular poem or story, he always has previous projects to finish off. He has to check **proofs** of books that are being prepared for publication. He has new projects to undertake, such as radio programmes to present. He can never switch off from his job, as he always has hundreds of ideas buzzing round his head.

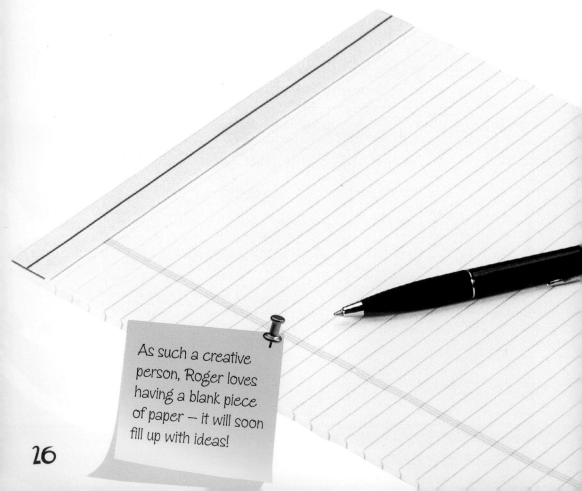

As such a creative person, Roger loves having a blank piece of paper — it will soon fill up with ideas!

Work in progress

If Roger is writing a story or a script, he works on a laptop computer. When he works with large amounts of text like this, it is great to be able to move things around on screen, because it is easy to make amendments, cuts, and additions.

However, when Roger is writing poetry, he always writes **longhand**. He does not like a poem to look too finished too soon. He enjoys watching a poem change and take shape, keeping all his crossings out and rewritten versions. When he considers a poem finally finished, he then types it up on his computer.

INSIDE INFORMATION

Roger's favourite poem is always the one he is working on. He finds the process of writing even more exciting than the thrill of reading a finished poem.

FIND OUT MORE...

Roger never sets out to write a poem that is specifically for young people or specifically for adults. He does not begin writing with anyone particular in mind. He just sets off with an idea and sees where the poetry takes him. Then when the poem is finished, Roger thinks about who will enjoy it most. Roger believes that ideas for writing come partly from our imaginations, but also from every other book, film, story, piece of music, or paiting that we have ever encountered. Every experience contains poetry – it is up to the writer to set it free.

THE GREAT SMILE ROBBERY

Main characters

Emerson .... our hero
PC Plod........................... a kindly copper
The Stinkers:
   Billy Bogie.................. a nose-picker
   Mrs Wobblebottom.... a greedy gannet
   Nick O'Teen .... a smelly smoker
   Sourpuss...................... a fleabitten moggy
   King Pong .... a grubby geezer

The plot

Emerson lives in a crazy world. The buses have rocket boosters so they can leapfrog over lorries and hurdle over bridges. Bank cashiers break into song and dance spontaneously and the government has a Minister for Happiness. Emerson owns a cupboard full of smiles – warmhearted ones, cheeky ones, straightforward "how do you do?" ones, shy ones, sad ones, and even a few that he's made up himself.

Every morning, he stands in front of the mirror and chooses a smile. Emerson's cheerful smiles make his neighbours feel warm and sunny – well, most of his neighbours. There's a gang of no-good, lousy layabouts at the bottom of the street who hate smiles. They are called the Stinkers.

Then the Minister for Happiness announces a competition to find the best smile in the land. The prize is to be the star of your very own television show! The Stinkers want to win. And they know just where they can lay their hands on a winning selection of smiles…

INSIDE INFORMATION

The Great Smile Robbery is a storybook, but there is plenty of poetry in it. Emerson's breakfast song, the song of the laughing cashiers, and the song of the Stinkers are obvious poems because of their rhythm and rhyme. Then there are the two-line rhyming descriptions about the Stinkers – each one is a short but vivid and very funny individual poem. The thirteen-line chapter entitled "All Over the Place" does not rhyme, but it has rhythm. This sort of poetry is called **free verse**. Have a close look at the story and see if you can spot any other types of poetry in it.

Roger
McGough

The
Great
Smile
Robbery

Illustrated by
Tony Blundell

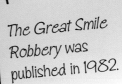

The Great Smile
Robbery was
published in 1982.

SKY IN THE PIE!

Themes

This whole poetry collection is full of surprises. Firstly, the poems are on a surprising range of subjects, including nature and the seasons, war and violence, animals and pets, music and sport, and many more. But what's even more surprising is the original way Roger treats all of these subjects, resulting in a huge variety of moods and emotions. For instance, *The Poet's Garden* is a vision of nature totally lacking in poetry! It surprises us by being totally the opposite of the descriptive, imaginative picture we expect from the title. On the other hand, *Out of Sight* appears to be a poem about an everyday, down-to-earth roadsweeper, which suddenly turns into a magical, imaginative event. *Tell Me Why?* at first seems to be a lighthearted, delightful riddle-based poem, until in a sudden twist near the end we realise it is a heart-wrenching goodbye from a father to his son before he goes off to war.

The poems in *Sky in the Pie!* will take you on a rollercoaster of emotions. Above all, they will entertain you.

Forms and rhyme schemes

Roger delights in playing with how a poem looks on the page. For instance, in *The New Poem (for 18 words)*, the words have not settled into the right order yet. He is skilled at writing **blank verse** – poetry with no regular rhythm – and also at using existing poetic forms.

One snowman poem is in the form of a **haiku**, a traditional Japanese poetic form that uses only three lines. In *A, A, B, B,* Roger pokes fun at being stuck in the habit of writing in rhyme. And in *People I'd Rather Not Talk About*, Roger leaves you to make up a rhyme for yourself!

INSIDE INFORMATION

The poem which gives this collection its title, *Sky in the Pie!*, warns us not to be set in our likes and dislikes, but to be open-minded when it comes to trying new things – to be prepared for surprises.

ROGER McGOUGH

SKY IN THE PIE

A BOOK OF POEMS

Sky in the Pie! was published in 1983.

AN IMAGINARY MENAGERIE

Themes

Have you heard of a brushbaby, a catapillow, or a teapet? Have you seen a chimp with a limp or elephants with smelly pants? Have you watched a flamingo flamenco or heard a newt play the flute? Have you encountered a yak wearing a yashmak and a baby gibbon with a bib on? If you enter *An Imaginary Menagerie*, be prepared to meet an alphabet of weird and wonderful animals, from A for allivator to Z for zonk!

Language

Roger does not write in a special, poetic sort of language. He uses everyday words that you might hear in normal conversation. Sometimes he even spells words to sound exactly the way people would say them – for example "neaver" for "neither".

However, in *An Imaginary Menagerie*, Roger runs riot with **wordplay**. He imagines anglefish to be triangle-shaped. He pictures daschunds dashing. He invents a myth about creatures called Goodgers who once lived in forests with Badgers. He renames warthogs as war thogs.

Roger also goes wild in this poetry collection with the rhythm and rhyme of words. There are wombats dressed for combat, oysters in cloisters, weasels at ease at easels, and a unicorn one misty moisty golden dawn forlorn upon a garden lawn!

INSIDE INFORMATION

Many of the poems in *An Imaginary Menagerie* are **nonsense verse**. Nonsense verse is poetry which is very funny and entertaining, although it has no logical meaning. There is a rich tradition of animal poems in nonsense verse. Among the earliest are Edward Lear's *The Owl and the Pussy-Cat* and *The Pobble Who Has No Toes*, and Lewis Carroll's *Jabberwocky* and *The Hunting of the Snark*, which date from the 1870s. At the turn of the 20th century, Hilaire Belloc's *The Bad Child's Book of Beasts* and *More Beasts for Worse Children* were hugely popular poetry collections for young people. More recently, Spike Milligan also wrote favourite animal nonsense poems such as *Silly Old Baboon* and *On the Ning Nang Nong*.

An Imaginary Menagerie was published in 1988.

RogeR McGough

An Imaginary Menagerie

BAD BAD CATS

Themes

In this collection, Roger's poems fall into three sections:
1) The Cats' Protection League – poems about a mob of gangster cats who are mad, bad and dangerous to know
2) Waxing Lyrical – imaginative, magical verses on a variety of subjects, with plenty of wordplay, fun and feeling
3) Carnival of the Animals – a parade of poems about birds and beasts, inspired by a musical work written by Camille Saint-Saëns in the 19th century.

Writing techniques

In *Vamoose*, Bugsy the gangster cat says "I soon be de Catfather". Roger is subtly suggesting a famous gangster film from the 1970s called *The Godfather*. Writers often refer to other writers, books or films in a disguised way, to bring other ideas into their work. This clever technique is called **allusion**. Can you spot any other allusions in the collection?

Roger's poem *Daffodils* is a cheeky, funny contrast to a famous poem about daffodils by William Wordsworth. A poem that jokily mimics another poem like this is called a **parody**.

In *Train Train* Roger writes as "I", which is called writing in the **first person**. At first, it is tricky to know who is speaking – are we listening to the thoughts of a person doing exercise training, or could it possibly be the thoughts of a train? In the end, we discover that it is a passenger on a train, thinking about exercise training! This is one of the reasons why Roger has been called "a trickster you can trust".

34

HAVE A GO

If you enjoy Roger's poems about naughty cats, why not try making up some of your own? For more inspiration, read *Old Possum's Book of Practical Cats* by TS Eliot, written in 1939. There are poems about a mischievous moggy named the Rum Tum Tugger, a gruesome twosome called Mungojerrie and Rumpelteazer, a magician called Mr Mistoffelees, a master criminal called Macavity the Mystery Cat, and Skimbleshanks the Railway Cat, among others. Or you could watch the musical based on Eliot's poems, named simply *Cats*. What other crazy cat characters can you create in rhyme and rhythm?

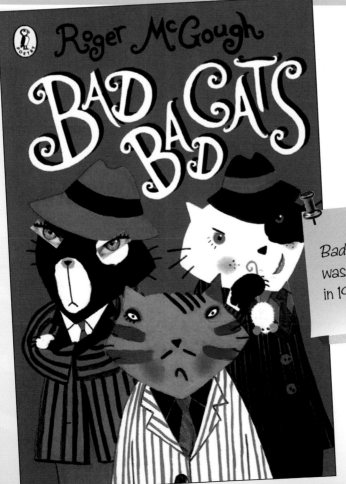

Bad Bad Cats was published in 1997.

35

PRIZES, POINTS OF VIEW, AND PRAISE

In his distinguished career, Roger has been awarded several honours from universities, including a professorship. He has also received two honours from the Queen – an OBE (Officer of the Order of the British Empire) in 1997 and a CBE (Commander of the Order of the British Empire) in 2005. Roger went to Buckingham Palace to collect his medals and is now entitled to put the letters CBE after his name. Roger has also been showered with prizes from the book world. He won the leading prize for children's poetry in Britain – the Signal Award – not once, but twice! Roger was awarded it in 1984 for *Sky in the Pie!* and again in 1999 for *Bad Bad Cats*. Roger also won the most prestigious prize for adults' poetry in Britain – the Cholmondeley Award – in 1999.

Roger with his wife and children after collecting his CBE at Buckingham Palace.

Rare honours

In 2001, Roger's beloved home town of Liverpool awarded him a very special honour called "the freedom of the city". Then in 2004, Roger was asked to write a poem to be included as part of a spectacular new fountain in the heart of Liverpool, in Williamson Square. Roger was delighted to have his words immortalised in a beautiful, busy part of his favourite city. If you are ever in Liverpool, make sure you to go to see it.

INSIDE INFORMATION

One of Roger's best tips for anyone who wants to be a poet is not to use the first rhyme that pops into your head. The first rhyme can be rather obvious and predictable, so it is not always the best one to choose.

A poem by Roger is inscribed around the edge of this spectacular fountain in Liverpool.

Super songs

Have you read the classic animal story, *The Wind in the Willows*, by Kenneth Grahame? In the early 1980s, Roger was approached by a theatre company who wanted to turn it into a musical show, with singing and dancing. The producer asked Roger to write the **lyrics**. The musical was first staged in Washington DC in the United States in 1984, then a year later transferred to Broadway in New York, where it was a huge hit. Roger's lyrics won a **nomination** for a famous American theatre award called a TONY!

HAVE A GO

HAVE A GO

If you would like to try songwriting, remember that you do not always have to start off with a tune. If you begin by composing a really rhythmic, rhyming poem, you will find that the words inspire their own melody later.

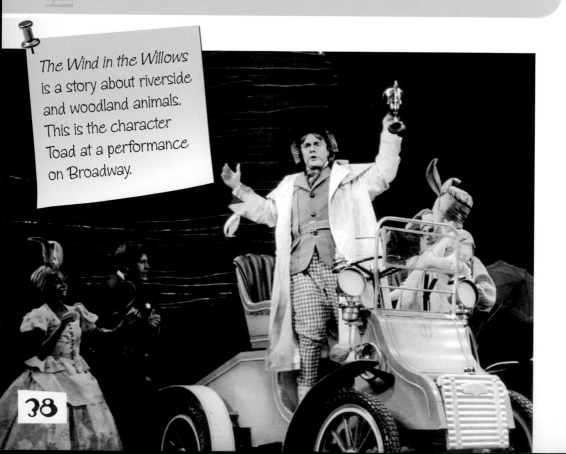

The Wind in the Willows is a story about riverside and woodland animals. This is the character Toad at a performance on Broadway.

Sight and sound

Roger has become as well-known and highly respected for his television, film and radio work as he has for his poetry. He has won two top awards called BAFTAs – one in 1985, for a children's film called *Kurt, Mungo, BP and Me*, and another in 1993 for a science film called *The Elements*. Roger was also asked to write the screenplays for animated film versions of two classic children's stories: Beatrix Potter's *The Adventures of Peter Rabbit* and Oscar Wilde's *The Happy Prince*. Today, you can hear Roger regularly on the radio as the presenter of BBC Radio 4's popular programme, *Poetry Please*.

Roger loves reading to his fans. He thinks it is one of the best things about being a poet.

Views in the news

When you are a famous poet like Roger, people called critics write their opinions of your work for newspapers and magazines. These are known as reviews. They are important because they help readers decide whether to spend their time and money on a book or not. Here is an example of a review for *Sensational!*, with some notes on how the critic has put it together. Would it encourage you to read the book?

Prepare for a vibrant carnival of sights, sounds, smells, tastes, and textures – *Sensational!* is a stunning anthology of poems inspired by the five senses.

a summary of what kind of book it is

The selection is the inspired choice of Roger McGough, best-selling poet and winner of both the Signal and Cholmondeley awards. Roger has included modern masterpieces from contemporary poets including Carol Ann Duffy and Michael Rosen, and treasures from the very best classic poets such as Wordsworth.

some background on the writer

the critic's opinion on whether it is a good or bad read, with clear reasons why

The rich variety of poetic forms, rhyme schemes, rhythm and language are as surprising and delightful as the wide-ranging subject matter. *Sensational!* is a thoroughly enjoyable read for all eight-year-olds and upwards, whether poetry fans or not. But beware – it is an eye-popping, nose-tickling, mouth-watering, skin-tingling, ear-splitting book!

a recommendation of who the critic thinks will like the book

Why not try writing your own review of a Roger McGough book or poem? You could give it to a friend who does not know it and see if they go on to read it. Ask them to write a review back, recommending one of their own favourite reads to you. You might discover a great new book, poem, or writer.

Pieces of praise

Here are some critics' opinions about Roger and his work:

" ...a word juggler who never misses a catch"
Charles Causley (poet)

" ...the patron saint of poetry"
Carol Ann Duffy (poet)

"He is a true original and more than one generation would be much the poorer without him"
The Times

"Liverpool's own Poet Laureate"
The Daily Post

Today, Roger does not go on many holidays because he often travels abroad for work. He regularly goes to other countries to do book tours and he sometimes also teaches on "poetry holidays", where he helps adults improve their writing skills in Grasse in the south of France. Whether away or at home, Roger's life revolves around poetry.

Roger's plans

Roger's wonderful writing career has spanned an amazing 50 years! You can find some of the finest poems he has written in a book called *All the Best*, and a mighty *Collected Poems* has also been published, gathering together every single poem Roger has written so far… Roger has plenty of ideas for more poems, plays and films in the future!

Roger goes on poetry trips to Grasse, in the south of France.

Writing in focus

Here's what some of Roger's many fans think of him and his work:

"Roger McGough is a master of rhyme and rhythm. The poems in *An Imaginary Menagerie* will twist your tongue up in knots!"

Alison, aged 11, from Coventry

"Roger's poems can make you laugh, cry, and think."

Eddie, aged 9, from Dumfries

"Roger McGough is the bees knees, the cat's whiskers, the big cheese!"

Sami, aged 8, from Liverpool

ROGER'S WISH LIST

Hopes...	Roger hopes that young people will improve the world for everyone. He is an optimistic person and has faith in the future.
Dreams...	Roger did not dream of being a writer when he was younger, but he thinks it is a lovely job to do and that he is very lucky doing it.
Ambitions...	Roger is very happy with his life and all he has achieved. His ambition is to keep writing for as long as possible – lucky for us!

TIMELINE

1937 Roger is born on 9 November in Seaforth, Liverpool.

1939–1945 World War II takes place.

1948 Roger goes to grammar school, called St Mary's College.

1955–1958 Roger studies at Hull University for a French and Geography degree. He decides he wants to be a poet, inspired by meeting the poets Philip Larkin and Christopher Logue.

1958–1959 Roger studies for a year to qualify as a teacher.

1959 Roger returns to Liverpool. He starts teaching at St Kevin's boys' school. He begins going to bars and clubs where other artistic people hang out, such as the poets Adrian Henri and Brian Patten. Roger starts giving entertaining readings of his work.

1963 Roger moves job to teach at Mabel Fletcher Technical College, all the time working on his poetry and giving performances. He moves in with painter/designer Thelma Monaghan.

1964 Roger gives up teaching to appear in a sketch/song/poetry group called The Scaffold on a weekly television programme called *Gazette*. Other television and theatre work follows. Roger writes his first theatre play: *Birds, Marriages and Deaths*.

1966 While continuing to write and perform, Roger takes a part-time teaching job at Liverpool College of Art.

1967 In March, Roger's poems appear in *The Liverpool Scene*. In May, his poems are published with those of Brian Patten and Adrian Henri in *The Mersey Sound*. In July, he has a poetry collection and novel published: *Summer with Monika* and *Frink*. In October, The Scaffold have a hit record with *Thank U Very Much*.

1970 Roger marries Thelma Monaghan.

1972 Roger and Thelma have a son, called Finn.

1973 The Scaffold breaks up and Roger becomes part of a new poetry/sketch/song group called Grimms. He also begins two years as Poetry Fellow at Loughborough University.

1974 Roger and Thelma have a second son, called Tom. Roger writes and presents for the children's educational television programme, *Focus*.

1975   Roger and Thelma split up.

1976   Roger falls in love with Hilary Clough and they move to Portobello Road, London.

1977   Roger's first children's book, *Mr Noselighter*, is published.

1979   A collection of poems for children by Roger and Michael Rosen is published, called *You Tell Me*.

1981   A poetry anthology for teenagers compiled by Roger, *Strictly Private*, is published.

1982   Another book for children, *The Great Smile Robbery*, is published.

1983   Poetry collection *Sky in the Pie* is published and wins the Signal Award.

1984   Roger writes the lyrics for an American musical version of the children's classic, *The Wind in the Willows*.

1986   Roger and Hilary's son, Matthew, is born.

1988   Poetry collection *An Imaginary Menagerie* is published.

1989   While continuing all sorts of writing, Roger becomes a presenter on BBC Radio 4's *Poetry Please* and also works on Granada TV's educational series for children, *Picture Box*.

1990   Roger and Hilary's daughter, Isabel, is born.

1991   Roger writes a film for television, *The Elements*, which later wins a BAFTA (British Academy of Film and Television Arts) award.

1997   *Bad, Bad Cats* is published and wins the Signal Award for Children's Poetry.
Roger writes children's theatre play, *The Sound Collector*.
Roger is awarded an OBE for services to poetry.

1999   Roger wins the Cholomondeley Poetry Award.

2001   Roger's home city honours him with "the Freedom of Liverpool".

2004   Roger writes a poem to be inscribed on a new fountain in Liverpool city centre.

2005   Roger is awarded a CBE.

FURTHER RESOURCES

More books to read

100 Best Poems for Children, Roger McGough (editor)
  and Sheila Moxley (illustrator) (Puffin Books, 2002)

All the Best: The Selected Poems of Roger McGough,
  Roger McGough and Lydia Monks (illustrator) (Puffin Books, 2004)

Tell Me About Writers and Illustrators: Roger McGough,
  Chris Powling (Evans Books, 2001)

Audiobooks

You can find some of Roger's work on CD and cassette, including:

Bad Bad Cats (read by Roger McGough) (Penguin Children's
  Audiobooks 1997)

Websites

Roger's official website:
  www.rogermcgough.org.uk

Roger is a presenter of the BBC radio programme *Poetry Please*:
  www.bbc.co.uk/radio4/arts/poetryplease.shtml

You can find out all about modern poetry and poetry events at:
  www.poetrysociety.org.uk

Disclaimer

All the internet addresses (URLs) given in this book were valid at the time of going to press. However, due to the dynamic nature of the Internet, some addresses may have changed, or sites may have ceased to exist since publication. While the author and publishers regret any inconvenience this may cause readers, no responsibility for any such changes can be accepted by either the author or the publishers.

GLOSSARY

allusion   disguised reference to something

anthology   collection of work by several different people

blank verse   poetry with no regular rhythm

catering   preparing food and drink for groups of people

editor   someone who oversees the words and content of a book

elocution   skill of speaking clearly, aloud to an audience

first person   to write in the first person is to write from the point of view of "I" or "we", rather than "he" or "she" or "they"

free verse   poetry which does not rhyme but which still has rhythm

haiku   traditional Japanese type of poem which has a fixed structure of only three short lines

hall of residence   place for students to live at a university

longhand   writing on paper with a pen or pencil rather than typing

lyrics   song words

Mass   main service held in Catholic churches

nomination   to be put forward for something, such as an award

nonsense verse   poetry which is written to make no sense

'O' level   exam that is equivalent to a modern GCSE

parody   something which mimics something else in a funny way

prep school   old-fashioned term for preparatory school

prisoner of war   someone who has been captured by their enemy during a war

proof   pages of a book that is being prepared for publication

reciting   speaking something aloud to an audience, often remembering it off by heart

rhythm   musical beat and pattern

rosary beads   prayer beads used by Roman Catholics

scholarship   prize of money to help a student pay the fees for a course of study

screenwriting   writing for television or film

tea-chest bass   home-made stringed instrument, made from an old tea chest and string

terrace   long row of similar houses joined together

warden   someone whose job is to look after a place where people live, and the people themselves

wordplay   using words in unexpected ways that are witty and amusing

INDEX